Indigenous

The beauty of this collection of poems is the way it uses every device capable of reaching the reader: starkly intense, almost confrontational black-and-white photographs; language that is at once direct yet deliberately not conversational; meter that invites ritual gestures; and verbal images that transport the reader to another time and culture. The result is a riveting immersion in all of what the term "indigenous" implies, with its suggestion of history—and time beyond, in a history with which few of us are familiar enough.

These poems go behind the familiar: Wounded Knee, the Trail of Tears, figures such as Sequoyah and Chief Joseph; past the artifacts, legends, and folkways encountered through reading and travels across America, to the intimate details of a specific family and their lives and world seen from the inside. These poems manage to braid together the members and traditions of a living family with the history of a country created, by force and guile, not in an empty wilderness awaiting discovery, but in a space teeming with viable nations in possession of arts, languages, customs, governments, and religions of their own. They give, as our literature seldom does, moral weight to the real and living representatives of those nations, rather than to the romanticized or demonized figures imagined by film.

They are important because they do what poetry does perhaps better than anything else: say what most of us find hardest to say about ourselves and our circumstances, not in political or sociological terms, but in the stories we tell ourselves in the solitude of our thought. And Reeser has clearly thought hard about the difficulty of keeping, at great personal cost—or even wanting to keep—an identity that complicates life; the importance of preserving our own names; the conflicted relationships between minorities and the majority, and among minorities struggling to advance; the ambivalent role of religion, and the ambiguity with which the faith of the majority may appeal to, but also repel, the descendants of people converted against their will. Some of the most moving poems in this collection are essentially highly original prayers, or warnings against Christianity issued by proudly resistant elders, or expressions of genuine devotion salted with ironic and clear-eyed disillusion.

Some few among the poems touch upon such relatively recent experiences as fighting in Vietnam as an American soldier, but bearing an indigenous name that recalls the Asian origin of Amerindian peoples. In "Thunderbird," a veteran's son recalls his father's military service this way:

> The Phan Rang fields first heard my foreign birth
> from helicopters hovering over Vietnam.

Another, "White Pocahontas," describes the unease of a mixed couple out for an evening together, attracting curious and probably hostile attention in a public place. And still others identify the poet's family members, in terms impossible not to recognize as one's own—universal—in the photographs that add so much to this document.

In all, *Indigenous* is more than simply a good read, or a compelling account of events we need to know better: it's an addition to our national literature by an accomplished poet who knows, and understands intimately, what she is so generously sharing in her work.

— Rhina P. Espaillat, author of *And After All*

JENNIFER REESER'S NEW BOOK OF POEMS, *INDIGENOUS,* provokes a strange sensation in the reader: an alien yet familiar landscape peopled with recurring characters, the mingling ghosts of history haunting the here and now and reanimating the myth and lore of her folk, both tragic and comic—as inseparable from Reeser's imagination as they are from her blood. Each poem enters into dialogue with the reader even as it maintains an ongoing conversation of sound and sense with the other poems in the collection, a steady, sturdy examination of essential tensions: what it means to be a descendant of the First Nations, an heir to Christian grace, and a poet writing in modern American.

"Poetry," Seamus Heaney says, "...whether it belongs to an old political dispensation or aspires to express a new one, has to be a working model of inclusive consciousness. It should not simplify. Its projections and inventions should be a match for the complex reality which surrounds it and out of which it is generated." This seems right, and Jennifer Reeser's *Indigenous* affirms its rightness not because her book is a grand manifesto on inclusiveness for its own sake, but because Reeser the poet seeks to be true to her poems as poetry, even as Reeser the person seeks to be true to the instincts, memories, heartbreaks, and victories that first gave rise to the poems:

> But I—I will return to water, lettuce,
> And vinegar, to sassafras and pepper,
> And treaties signed by those with little English,
> But whose inherent language is forgotten
> And bids me to recall and resurrect it.

Measured syllables and tribal pulses punch back and forth throughout Reeser's newest collection of verse. Already a master of poetic forms, Reeser has reapplied her talent in what amounts to a major development in her repertoire, bringing the reader to that Native American borderland of the heart that has apparently been a major part of her life, but a part we've only seen in glimpses up to now. Upon engaging the poems of *Indigenous,* the reader crosses into that borderland with English rhymes and Western meters serving as our compass points. The reader experiences the psychological landscape of *Indigenous* through the same flint-cut purity of style that has defined Reeser's poetry since *An Alabaster Flask* first appeared a decade and a half ago.

Reeser has always had a keen ability to lead us through her poetry to show us not only what to see but also how to look. *Indigenous*

gives us a fresh set of tracks; each poem on the page leads us out beyond ourselves, enticing with equal parts confidence and risk, generosity and endurance. Reeser repurposes the sonnet to prevail and multiply throughout *Indigenous* as a studied and pensive series of interrelated cantos celebrating her Native American legacy. A villanelle in Reeser's hands becomes a bittersweet dirge for what is lost; and a rondeau explodes with a new pattern of colors as a dance of joy for all that can and (if Jennifer Reeser has anything to do with it) will be rescued, retained and—like the poems that make up *Indigenous*—remembered for years to come.
   — Joseph O'Brien, poetry editor of the *San Diego Reader*

INDIGENOUS

poems

JENNIFER REESER

ABLE MUSE PRESS

Copyright ©2019 by Jennifer Reeser
First published in 2019 by

Able Muse Press

www.ablemusepress.com

All rights reserved. No part of this book may be used or reproduced in any manner whatsoever without written permission except in the case of brief quotations embedded in critical articles and reviews. Requests for permission should be addressed to the Able Muse Press editor at editor@ablemuse.com

Printed in the United States of America

Library of Congress Control Number: 2018931411

ISBN 978-1-77349-023-6 (paperback)
ISBN 978-1-77349-018-2 (digital)

Cover image: "Feathered Court" by Alexander Pepple

Cover & book design by Alexander Pepple

Able Muse Press is an imprint of *Able Muse:* A Review of Poetry, Prose & Art—at www.ablemuse.com

Able Muse Press
467 Saratoga Avenue #602
San Jose, CA 95129

In devoted memory
of my beloved grandfather,
Claude Griffin
C.G.
"Monk" Maiden

Do na da go huhn i
ᎠᏔᎴᏍᏗ

—*I will see you again*

Acknowledgments

I am grateful to the editors of the following journals where many of these poems originally appeared, sometimes in earlier versions:

Able Muse, Angle, Autumn Sky Poetry Daily, Levure Litteraire, Life and Legends, Mezzo Cammin, the *National Review,* the *San Diego Reader, and TRINACRIA.*

Contents

x   Acknowledgments

I. The Ancients

5   Enigma
8   Not Stifled by the Ground
9   FNU: First Name Unknown
10 One Un-delayed Way
11 Apache Park
12 On a Portrait of Chief Joseph
14 ᎡᏊᎬᎢ
15 Nature Does Not Care
16 The Civil Execution of Joshua Martin
19 Cherokee Prayer
20 Three Seneca Chiefs to George Washington
21 Jacob Surber, Indian Spy
23 To Mahala
24 Why the Cherokee Abandoned Privilege
26 Great Grandmother Ora

II. Lore

- 29   Thunderbird
- 30   A Doll Lace Monk
- 32   Monk Returns to Speak of Mountains
- 33   The One That Got Away
- 36   My brother's arrowheads
- 38   Veterans' Victory Rite
- 40   "No, not the monkey, Mother, but the stag . . ."
- 41   To Treat the Child's Disease
- 42   Black Flies and Berries
- 44   Chickasaw Plum
- 45   Between the Creek
- 46   Indian Angel
- 47   Perhaps My Patmos
- 49   Raised on Rogers
- 51   Cherokee Love Charm
- 54   Not Quite Gods
- 55   Spearfinger
- 58   To Lonely Lots
- 59   Made in America

III. Blazing the Trail

- 63   Sapphics for Sequoyah
- 64   I Have No Drum
- 65   The Griffin
- 67   I Have No Bow
- 68   No Beatrice Am I

- 69 Redfoot on the Trail of Tears
- 70 How Many Perished?
- 71 Five Fly Skyward
- 72 Tired Blood to Colonel Hawthorne
- 73 This Primitive Rain Dance
- 74 Angry Indian Lover
- 75 White Pocahontas
- 76 The Water Cannibals
- 78 Wounded Knee
- 80 Ka No Gi S Di Asks the Amorous Commander
- 81 To Melissa Honey Bee, Who Has Hidden My Feathers in a Dream
- 82 I Have No Horse
- 83 On a Plane Going East
- 84 Half-breed
- 85 The Jealous She-Raccoon among Garbage Cans
- 86 On an Antique Photograph of My Martin Aunts
- 87 Navajo and Cherokee

IV. Homeland

- 91 At Cahokia Indian Mounds
- 93 Aqua, Turquoise, and Teal
- 94 The Rivers of the Navajo
- 96 Weep with the Waters
- 98 Song of the Long-Hair Clan
- 99 In Tulsa
- 101 Supply Package for Sacred Stone Camp
- 103 A Sioux Protest

V. Prophesies

- *107*   The Chosen One
- *108*   The Arrowhead
- *109*   They Won't Remove Me
- *110*   We Told You So
- *111*   Red Jacket to the Seneca, on Religion
- *112*   Rinse My Sins
- *113*   A Wail from the Wild Potato Clan Arbor
- *114*   The Flute My Father Gave
- *115*   They Won't Erase Me
- *116*   How to Hide the Native
- *117*   Cherokee Childbirth Chant
- *118*   The Charts and Wheels
- *119*   O Great Spirit
- *120*   Benediction

- *127*   Notes

Indigenous

I. The Ancients

Enigma

Grandfather works his crosswords at the table,
While I—distracted from my Aesop fable—
Attempt to guess his task, but am unable.

The cuckoo clock above him, on the eights,
Keeps rhythmic timing, lifting pinecone weights
Of lead chains, while the bird bursts through its gates.

I grimace at the grinding of the lead.
The salmon walls behind his vivid, red
Complexion glow around his coal-black head.

Black glasses rim the ears. He boasts a shave
As close as that of some ancestral brave
Whose notice the unmarried maidens crave.

I finish "reading," wait for him to say
My name in that peculiar, rasping way
I hear inside my own head, to this day,

Too young to recognize or understand
The motive for these motions of his hand,
Or what the puzzle architects have planned;

While Jesus—blond and white—elicits feeling,
Portrayed in paint, perpetually kneeling
Beside His rock, gaze raised up to the ceiling.

But Grandfather keeps his silence, like a hawk
Prepared to swoop. This is his daily walk
Of mind, away from sound, and idle talk.

Befitting a stern man of humble means,
His typic meal of cucumber, cornbread, beans,
And coffee waits, beside seed magazines.

The pieces of his verbal puzzle dance
Invisibly—no mindless game of chance—
To Perry Como's lyrics of romance

Or captured, falling stars, in easy pitch.
A tall, plaid thermos meets his knee, from which
Throughout the day, he pours the liquid rich

With bitter chicory, filling the inside
Of hefty cups—substantial, shallow, wide
And white as the adornments of a bride.

And I am mesmerized. I cannot tear
My eyes away from his un-graying hair,
Bowed over this obsession we both share.

Though, if I were to turn aside and look,
Examining each corner, every nook
And walnut shelf, to open every book,

His signature—in black ink—would appear:
Diagonal initials, in a tier
Would mark the published annals of each year;

The illustrated dictionaries sold
One hundred years within the past, so old
I fear the leaves would not survive a fold;

His cherished Zane Grey novels, strangely sketched
With noble native heroes, would be etched,
Across each flyleaf, eloquently stretched—

Possessive to a startling degree.
He finishes his challenge, finally,
And offers his warm coffee cup to me.

His grip allows not one drop to be spilt.
His black eyes—fierce in youth—enlarge and tilt.
I rise without reluctance from my quilt.

His fingertips smell mildly of ink.
Dust motes revolve around him, glowing pink.
To draw his spirit into mine, I drink.

Not Stifled by the Ground

"Take care," you told my father, "of my girls,"
Mere moments from the time you would depart.
To think on it, the melancholy curls
Like vapor in the lungs, to choke my heart.
Administering, though, that admonition,
Before the man you came to call your son
Despite so little time, a new tradition
Began from you—and not the only one.
But when you slipped from that hospital room,
You did not realize, your spoken pearl
Would be repeated, to my waiting groom,
Who then would pass it on, for my own girl.
For centuries to come, let it resound,
Your voice not stifled—ever—by the ground.

FNU: First Name Unknown

Native American Female, Unknown Name
Eight generations ago was my great grand dame,

There in a line I assumed to be whiter than snow:
English and Scottish were evident. Powhatan? No.

Told of the presence of this unpredicted Dark Horse,
Rather than standing in awe, I acknowledge, *Of course*.

Savage and strange as the Jamestown address, and vague years—
Hundreds between us—arises the family name: *Spears*.

Paper Doll Powhatan, comes the unfortunate phrase—
Firm in my thinking, firm as far off are the days;

Joining the ranks of the ancients and modern ones, those
Nobles and commoners both, who revive and make rose

Feeling and face at the same time, without and within,
Feeding the bloom of my spirit, with that of my skin.

Holding this mystery intimately, I sigh, "Ho,
Here is a Maiden of meaning—my white buffalo."

Native American Female, First Name Unknown:
Rare, in her line; now, inside me, and never alone.

One Un-delayed Way

A cretic hymn entirely in Cherokee sounds

Smoky meats stowed away
Long ago, making you
Slow, you go loading hay—
Neatly, mutely—duty due.

What a day! What loosed heat!
Oh—(ha!)—not one young, wee
Yew was cut. Loading wheat
Late, you quote Donne to me.

Unseen neigh, unknown squeal
Take you home—healing, low—
Who won't see, who won't steal,
Who won't lay you to woe.

Oak one day may, too, one
Un-delayed way, no yaw
Taking you, lost, to none—
Squat to eat, soon to gnaw.

Apache Park

As I was on my daily evening walk
Around the pathways of Apache Park,
A lone, white feather—like a comb of chalk—
Towards me drifted down the humid dark,
Down from the boughs of live oak overhead.

I stopped, stood still, and caught it in mid-air
As though it symbolized a loved one dead,
Returning with a white plume in his hair.

Until I reached the entry of my home,
It rested, hidden tightly in my hand—
More precious than bright relics brought from Rome;
Mysterious, yet natural; unplanned
But orchestrated somehow, and exact
In search of me—both fantasy and fact.

On a Portrait of Chief Joseph

A monolith of common sense and stricture,
Descended from the people of Nez Perce,
Grandfather Neeley hung Chief Joseph's picture
Above the famous quote, so like a verse

Of undisputed poetry, I enter
The sleeping room as though it were a church,
A portrait of Saint Peter at its center,
Or like I would the lightning-scarred white birch

Ojibwe say we got from Thunderbird
When Waynaboozhoo—son of streaming air—
Stole a single spark of fire, and stirred
The ire of him who had refused to share.

In other words, as though some sacred bark
Surrounded me, beside the quilted bed
Where white chenille illuminates the dark,
Reminding me, I stand before the dead.

This sentence—so sublime, I cannot sever
Its meaning from the sound of falling water:
"My chieftains, I shall fight no more forever,"
Without one scalp, one brave, one senseless slaughter.

A golden, oval, antique frame encloses
the fur-trimmed braids against his necklace bands,
no evidence of those acclaimed pierced noses
on Joseph's words, "From where the sun now stands...."

The phrase stills and allays this bloody war
Inside of me, between the Red and White.
No foot of either race can run before,
"I'm tired. No more—forever—will I fight."

ᎡᎶᎩᎢ

Someday, should I say savagely, *Guh gay yoo hee,*
Perhaps at last you will have found a cause to flee,
But lay away your temperate anxiety.
I am of the Five Civilized, so listen civilly,
Before I turn to journey west, from Tennessee;
Before you travel, having seized my world from me
By slow degrees, through proper channels, legally.
"I love you" is its paraphrase from Cherokee.

My ululations were not meant to augment fear,
Nor were my invocations of strange apparition,
Nor were my drums of war, nor my flute's peaceful sound.
But little alters through my people's eons here.
As you repudiate my sad and fierce tradition,
I go, though lacking gaiety in promised ground.

Nature Does Not Care

Nature does not care what we believe,
By what way we were formed, nor how we feel.
Look in my face, blood brother, see and grieve
Or joy, that our umbilical is real.
I shall not draw you from the powwow dance.
I will not bore with silly inquiries,
Nor interrupt the ceremonial chants
Through which you thrill the pretty, British tease.
Off, in the shadows, half lit, unobtrusive
I shall remain, a sister to the smoke,
With changing features—childlike and elusive,
With chalky power you may not invoke.
I will not ask you how, nor what it means.
The answer is not learned, but in my genes.

The Civil Execution of Joshua Martin

Missouri, 1863

Suspended in star-vacant space,
Grandmother Osage Moon appears.
Illuminating out his face,
Grandfather Martin's fifty years.
Increasing in his feral ears,
The calling of a common loon
Attendant on Grandmother Moon
Forewarns his senses—though too late,
For soldiers are arriving soon,
When he will fall at his front gate.

He comes from that inherent race
The *New York Times* reviewer smears
Eight years preceding, to debase
The Amerind before his peers,
Employing typeface to impugn,
To render as a crude cartoon
The Red Man, and to underrate,
Encouraging that fatal swoon,
When he will fall at his front gate.

Near Joshua, mindful of his place,
Stock-still, filled with a young son's fears,
Caleb Columbus stares, to trace
Approaching forms on stark frontiers.
Aggression drapes their shoulders, strewn
As though to mimic Daniel Boone;
As though they rode a rude, slave state.
They shoot, as at some mean raccoon,
When he will fall at his front gate.

Hiding its grimace, in disgrace,
Indigenous vision dries and clears.
His loved ones kneel to Earth, embrace
Their means of life with native tears,
To sing for him an ancient tune,
And move entire tribes to croon
With crimson faces, stern and straight.
They summon forth the world commune
When he will fall at his front gate.

Yet no one threatens, nor gives chase,
Nor hurls blunt axes, nor sharp spears,
With rapid passion, passed apace
By vapid spite and vicious cheers.
The mounted murderers maroon
His corpse, to seek a cool saloon,
To eat and drink, and proudly prate
And tell the tale—from night till noon—
When he will fall at his front gate;

To flirt with European lace,
With pretty eyes, and prying beers,
Returning finally to base—
One medal more, to their careers.
My forebear's middle-aged cocoon
Will look no more on their platoon,
But dignified by pain, sedate,
Will move like wind across a dune,
When he will fall at his front gate.

Ancestor, rise again! Festoon
Yourself with horn, become immune,
Defeating death, to make your Fate
A maple, by a hatchet hewn,
When *he* will fall, at *his* front gate.

Cherokee Prayer

Great Spirit, who has made each race,
Look kindly on the human brood;
Remove the hate and arrogance
Which hinder us from brotherhood.

Three Seneca Chiefs to George Washington

    December, 1790

    We ask each other, what could we have done
    To warrant such unfeeling punishment?
    Your goodness, so they said, shines bright as sun.

    Attention! We communicate as one.
    Great Father, open hearts are what we meant.
    We ask each other, what could we have done?

    You boasted you could crush us down to none.
    We gave great ground, demanding not one cent!
    Your goodness, so they said, shines bright as sun.

    The English called you children with no gun,
    Deceiving us—but we are innocent.
    We ask each other, what could we have done?

    Your anger's course against us must be run.
    Your fury, Father, surely now is spent.
    Your goodness, so they said, shines bright as sun.

    They told us you were weak—but you have won.
    Appealing to your spirit, we relent.
    We ask each other, what could we have done?
    Your goodness, so they said, shines bright as sun.

Jacob Surber, Indian Spy

Why, my distant ancestor, has none spoken
Ever once extolling your name in writing—
Either as a hero, or as a token?
You deserve epics.

Jacob Surber, Indian spy and rebel—
Too fantastic or overly familiar
Lies Virginia's gray Shenandoah pebble,
Quaint beyond telling.

Frayed to quick antiquity's aqua polish
Live the maverick hills and lavish valleys—
Soon persuading the artist to demolish
All but the vision.

Who does justice to such romantic scenery?
Norman Rockwell, when imitating Titian,
Tracing red through both suave and savage greenery,
Might be successful.

Jacob Surber, grandfather, mole—appearing
Now within my informed imagination,
Light and shadow compete within a clearing
Over your features.

Native agent, after your own kind, under
Springtime orders coming from Captain Denton,
You are freely ranging through mountain thunder,
Killing your brothers.

Here inside me, your genes, your motivation
Move anew, reporting to far Fort Wendall—
Bringing forth a rebellious, newborn nation,
Volunteer, ever;

Wounding, taking prisoners, next dispersing
Tories, marching to the Burnt Ordinary,
You surrender never. I hear you cursing
Despot and bondage;

Shot by musket ball in the left-side shoulder,
Shaking hands with Washington after Yorktown—
Fading while indigenous winds grow colder,
Spare as a specter.

To Mahala

Mahala, your inclining, cinnabar eyes
Accuse me from the mirror, as I blink
Away Grandfather's tears, to brush my pink
Complexion with the "paint" this sponge applies.
The Cherokee and Osage cheekbones rise,
Even as your mouth's sharp corners sink:
Respectful, regal, tragic. Do you think
White Lily will approve them, or despise?
I squeeze the bottle and replace the stopper
Of screen whose sixth ingredient is cetyl,
Ensuring that the contents will not harden,
To keep my skin from deepening to copper—
Our native shade, and most beloved metal.
Grandmother—grace my face, and grant your pardon.

Why the Cherokee Abandoned Privilege

At one time, there had been a privileged sect,
A-Ni' Qua-Ta'-Ni, whom some elders say
Presaged the Cherokee, with great respect,
While some dismiss it outright, with dismay.

Perhaps this long-ago society
Conceived, constructed, and preserved the mounds,
But perished through some weird calamity—
The constant fire extinguished, or wild hounds;

Or pestilence destroyed them, with one blow,
Each hallowed priest, each mystic minister
Drowned in a cataclysmic flood or snow—
Though some claim something much more sinister.

These were the "sanctified," those set aside
And given preference, given supervision
Of ceremony, who performed with pride
The ancient rites, in unsurpassed precision.

Superior, the tribesmen would suppose,
Above and superseding any other,
Till one rogue, misbehaving priest arose
To take the wife of their chief's own brother.

Akin to Brahmins, they—through birthright "law"—
The *Nicotani*, held as though by rein
The people, in rare reverence and awe,
And thus, grew fat with rudeness and disdain.

They had ascended and none could discover
Their means of massacre, nor where they're buried.
A lovely woman they would make a lover—
Even the shrinking maid, even the married.

The tribe endured with brooding for a time
Each new atrocity from this high caste,
Each overbearing insolence and crime,
Until a daring brave appeared at last,

The son of an authoritative man
Avenging the dishonor of his wife,
Who led the Cherokee to kill the clan,
Not sparing any Nicotani life.

Not since that bloodbath do the Cherokee
Exalt a single soul, nor tolerate
Entitlement by birth—society
Admitting neither paramount nor great.

Great Grandmother Ora

Taking raw cowhide and fashioning purses,
Skillfully turning out wallets and belts,
Tanned leather shoes—the way I might make verses—
Ora created; like white women's felts

Turned into quilts. My great-grandmother Martin,
Blind from an eye disease no one could cure,
Made them by personal darkness, near Tartan
Neighbors who purchased her Native allure.

Generous, giving, diminutive, *filthy*,
Grandmother called her, with all of her clan,
Yet—in the end—in her inner world, wealthy,
Able to wed a white, prosperous man.

Last in my line to bear witness to ritual
Old as Methuselah—older perhaps—
Ora, my ancestor, clung to the Natural
Order more aged than Columbus's maps.

All I have left of her lives in a portrait.
Reader, you see, the one here in my book.
Docile, her sightless eyes downcast and dormant,
This is the last formal portrait she took.

Beauty is evident, still, in her features.
Almond, upturned are her blank, Native eyes.
Pity is evident, too, for those creatures
Kind but unclean, whom the buyers despise.

II. Lore

Thunderbird

The Phan Rang fields first heard about my foreign birth
From helicopters hovering over Vietnam.
My father nicely hidden from a hostile bomb,
Was told through rasping speakers on the crisping earth.
That news, which should have cheered, left little room for mirth,
Revealing his position in the rice and palm
Between Bandito Charlie and Ohio Tom,
While calling into question its announcer's worth.
Strategically incautious, at the very least;
A sentimental act of indiscretion—
How could such a lapse in judgment have occurred?
I hope perhaps to be a signal to the East
That here was one whose fate would fall to its possession,
Whose name came through the heavens from a Thunderbird.

A Doll Lace Monk

"Monkey," they nicknamed my grandfather Maiden,
Born in the year of the Monkey, like me—
Nineteen-oh-eight, in late Cherokee country,
Cowled by the mountains of east Tennessee.

Shortened to "Monk," it would be, as he sprouted.
Now in the Cherokee tongue, it's a long word
Voiced in phonetics, "Ah-DAH'-li-s-gee-YEECE'-gee."
Use of a nickname so long is absurd.

Thus, should a Native address him, "A doll lace"—
Nasal and sing-song—would come out, instead.
Papaw's dark mother attired him in ascots—
Just as if born to some lord, British-bred.

Heard as "a doll lace," the phrase was deceptive,
Leading an English-immersed girl or boy
Wrongly to reckon he was a companion
Named for the trim on a "feminine" toy.

Cherokee, though, had been strictly forbidden,
Punishable by a rap on the knuckle.
Teacher corrected with, "Ora!" or "Josie!"
Never with "Feather!" or "Young Honeysuckle!"

Hiding their guttural, candid expressions,
Cherokee voices were smothered with shame.
Faced with the discipline practiced by devils,
Who would have translated Grandfather's name?

No one. And yet, how appropriate, fitting.
Always in silk socks and dress shoes, how formal
Grandfather was! A white handkerchief ever
Present to cough in—as though it were normal.

Always a shirt of impractical whiteness.
"No dirty Indian," they seemed to say—
Laundered, pressed, folded, and smelling of greenness,
Finely defying the stinking cliché.

Monk Returns to Speak of Mountains

Returning to converse with me in dreams,
His torso draped with cotton rib, to slouch
Familiarly against the worn, rolled seams
And flattened cushions of his old, tweed couch,
He lit up at my question: "Do you still
Long for the mountain, Papaw?" And each hand
Upraised at once, a sudden look of thrill
Across his face, to indicate how grand
In scope those hills, how great his love, his hair
So raven as to be a boy's, he said,
"The mountain—yes!" Then nodded, "It is there!"
Then, forearms stiffening, his fingers spread,
He gestured in a mid-air sketch, as though
To shape its outlines: "Where it is, you know!"

The One That Got Away

The Bird Clan—raven, dove, and eagle—
Is Mother's clan. It is through her
My lineage is counted legal,
And I am called a Messenger.

And though our arbor happens near
To left, on ceremonial land,
Of that "delivery" clan, the Deer,
We do not carry news, by hand.

But we, we keepers of the Bird—
Two groves from those who keep the sod—
Come out with the unspoken word
Between humanity and God.

The blowgun and the hunting snare
We handle with uncommon skill;
And we alone may reap from air—
The sole collectors of the quill.

Forty moons ago, I ran—
My ribbons following behind
In strands of long hair—from a man
Whose treatment of me was unkind.

He was a white man, old and fat—
Though once, they say, he had good looks.
He wore a curved-brimmed, Texas hat,
And said that he had read great books.

Enamored of the fire stick,
He laid a claim to classic letters—
But this insistence was a trick.
In truth, he leads those pale go-getters

Who mock the word and bleed the weak,
Who blow—like powder—what they read;
Whose tongues, divided when they speak
With skilled maliciousness, mislead.

I saw the fairness of their skin,
Desirous to assume as sure
The fairness of their souls within—
But those were filthy, and impure.

They aided wild Atakapas
Who gnawed men's flesh with grisly rite,
In regions where the Mardi Gras
Is greeted as a feast of light.

I trusted each. I called him "friend"
Who never was a friend to me,
Who only took. And in the end,
They placed me in a pillory.

One sunset, then another sun,
He bided time, through their abuse,
Then—feigning valor—dropped his gun,
Insisting that they let me loose.

With half-despair, and half-conceit,
Though overflowing faith, I fled
The one who boasted that he beat
And then abandoned me for dead.

I fled, to fly with birds of prey,
With birds of peace, and live to tell
More cunningly than he can say,
The best revenge is living well.

My brother's arrowheads

affixed, each, to a saw-toothed blade,
invisibly adhering, three
of modest size and weighty grade,
alike in form, appeal to me.

Across my brother's face appears
his great-grandmother's dignified
expression, that the Trail of Tears
perfected, as she walked and cried.

Because he has unearthed this wealth
of prehistoric artifacts
himself: by diligence and stealth,
collecting arrow, spear and ax.

By offering to me these gifts,
from which he claims I have my choice,
my clear enthusiasm lifts
his spirits, with a passive voice.

Archaic Dovetails, Bifurcates—
indented sharp tangs at their base—
appraise us from the metal plates
where eons at a glance take place.

A fluted Clovis spearhead hangs
upright—its pressured channel flake
entices me with inner pangs.
But this is one I cannot take.

Too valued, for this man to lose.
Of all these paragons, his best.
I realize he would not refuse—
aloud or mutely—my request.

The quartz and flint Archaic trio—
a Side Notch arrowhead, by cast—
I finger: store enough of geo-
logic power from the past.

Ten thousand years of time I hold
at long last, and the worth thereof—
not any trouble to enfold
when braided with a brother's love.

Veterans' Victory Rite

> An ancient Cherokee shaman's formula for war, translated

Song for the adversary

Hey! You! Listen! Now do we
Lift red ward clubs instantly.
Soon his soul shall lack for motion,
There beneath the earth and ocean,
Where the clubs of war take aim
Like black ball bats in the game;
There, his living soul shall be,
Nevermore again to see.
Hey! We cause it to be so,
Never shall his spirit go
Lifting up the war club. We
Cause it to be so, to be.
Where the war club and black cloud
Come together in a shroud,
Underneath our mother ground,
Never shall it move around,
Lifted to allow him seeing.
We have called it into being.

Song for the warriors

Instantly, their souls shall be
In the seventh heaven, free.
Never shall their souls be broken.
This shall happen. We have spoken.
We have moved their souls hereby
To a place of peace on high.
Crimson war clubs as their guard,
Never shall their souls be scarred.
Cause it quickly to be so.
There on high, their souls shall go.
Grant now they will not grow blue,
Shielded by red war clubs. Yu!

"No, not the monkey, Mother, but the stag . . ."

"No, not the monkey, Mother, but the stag,"
She says to me, and pierces through my ear
The steel post of a golden-antlered deer
Which mirrors that upon my shoulder bag.
"That is your spirit." Fabric patterns zag
In zebra prints around us. Leopard spots appear—
The creatures of Rwanda and Zaire.
Behind her words, the seconds seem to lag.
Here is a novel view with which to cope:
For her, I am fragility and grace—
The esoteric watcher in the wood,
The neutral mover. *Bambi Antelope.*
I tell myself, "Pull your poker face.
Your fawn has followed you and understood."

To Treat the Child's Disease

An ancient Cherokee shaman's formula, translated

Listen! Quickly you've drawn near,
O Blue Sparrow-Hawk, to hear!
Quickly you descend to rest
In the arbor's spreading crest.
An intruding bird alone
Is this shadow on him shown.
Swooping, swift, you carry it away.
Remedy has been accomplished. Hey!

Listen! Quickly do you draw
Nearer, O Brown Rabbit-Hawk!
From your rest upon a bough,
Speedily you come down now.
Only for committee blather
Do these feathered creatures gather.
You scatter them without delay.
Remedy has been accomplished. Hey!

Black Flies and Berries

Four sisters and a single brother gather
In Osage country, nineteen-thirty-eight.
They catch black flies, then, with the insects, slather
Berries, and make their mother sit up straight.

Old Mattie's life is ending. *May she walk
On strongly*, so the siblings' efforts say.
Her skin—pink-gold in youth—has turned to chalk.
She dies in summer, child born New Year's Day.

The son applies an elbow to her spine
Between each fragile, native shoulder blade
Pulled by his sisters, forcing her to dine
Upon the foul refreshment they have made:

Black flies and berries. Family members leave
The room—disgusted by the cryptic rite,
Escaping from the stifling heat, to grieve
In private, by the fresh air of the night.

My grandfather is among them. Grandma Mary
Katherine stays behind, the "diplomat"
Who wonders at the sense behind the berry
So different from her English habitat;

Unlike her husband, feeling seized and trapped.
Her mind—quick and extraordinarily nimble—
Is like the black flies, rapid to adapt,
And with the flies and berries, be a symbol.

First, for life, itself. If that should fail,
And if their ritual of the fruit and flies
Deters not Death, but Mattie turns more pale
Tomorrow, rolls onto the floor and dies,

This ritual will mean a smooth transition—
The black flies signifying newer birth
When carefully combined with the fruition
Of sweets collected from a vernal Earth.

Observe the ghastly black flies as they hover
Over the crimson berries, thick as oil—
And know, Old Mattie never will recover.
My kin will bare their brown feet to the soil

The day they bury her, the warm and stony
July terrain a "touchstone" where they bury,
Blending white and Indian ceremony,
To shock the town, and baffle Grandma Mary.

Chickasaw Plum

Mother Rose, to spite Aunt Plum,
    Has cut my lengths of fine, straight hair,
Between her finger and her thumb,
    Then combed her curls with finer care.

That darling of the Chickasaw
    Bore twigs to blossom in my braids,
Whose scent delighted my Papaw
    In varied, violet, valley shades.

The European pear, instead,
    She left to me, on which to lean—
Ashamed and shorn—my maiden head,
    Spotted, bottom-heavy, green.

See my sister, Bee. She shows
    That which shears do not allow,
Shortened lock, with thickened nose,
    Shovel tooth and sloping brow.

Rose shall always be the chief
    Of the mountain, bog, and pass:
Budding hip and turning leaf,
    Maple, birch, and sassafras.

Between the Creek

Between the Oklahoma Creek
And Cherokee, I lived my life,
Betrothed to Jesus Christ, but wed
The pale son of a preacher's wife.

My ninth grandfather was so dark
And Powhatan, that "Black" became
For Trader Robert Davis, more
Familiar than his proper name.

So swarthy was my sweet firstborn—
A faded, copper, one-cent coin—
His father's mother hinted that
He issued from a different loin.

I was the dirty Indian
Out of the cypress swamp, who bore—
Without the white man's medicine—
Her babies on the flowered floor;

As had been Father's father's mother,
Blind Ora, Watie's woman clone.
None other than instinctive stock
Exists so distant and unknown.

Indian Angel

I howled, I howled, the night he passed away
And left me to the lover and the louse.
Moroser than a mother or a spouse,
Immobile in his daughter's arms I lay—
Terrified that his willful spirit may
Not come with me, nor leave that vacant house
Devoted to the moth ball and the mouse.
But no. Behind and over, as I pray,
He stands, and listens while the morning song
In Iroquois is loosened from my tongue.
And though I've been mistaken all along,
No sermon does he preach, that I was wrong,
But only shifts in shape—first old, then young,
Once sage, next in a rage; now meek, now strong.

Perhaps My Patmos

Blue glass like Heaven—I may not revisit
To glimpse you hovering above the altar,
Nor go to water underneath your panels.

I may not seat myself upon your benches,
On velvet cushions edged by hand-rolled piping.

I will not sneeze and sniffle when those ladies
Pass by, their overpowering, floral perfume—
Taboo, like unseen, fluid totems—wafting
In trails throughout the peaceful sanctuary.
Not one more time will any see me enter.

Your streetside doors are locked, forbidding entry.
Your women bar me from the morning worship,
And say there is no room, and show me into
A nursery, soon to fill with little children
Whose keeping I am given, till their mothers
Replace their ink pen caps and close the pages
On First Corinthians or Revelation.
(How much I longed to study that prophetic
And enigmatic chapter charged with wonder!)

Those round-hipped, sweetly-scented, milky women
Will draw their shawls around their sloping shoulders,
Will lift their blue- or green-eyed sons and daughters
With animated kisses, off the carpets
Where we have waited for them, Indian-sitting.

As I replace a silver-feathered earring,
Each obviously Dutch or German lady
Will journey home to her Italian husband
To costume for an evening at the opera.

But I—I will return to water, lettuce,
And vinegar, to sassafras and pepper,
And treaties signed by those with little English,
But whose inherent language is forgotten
And bids me to recall and resurrect it.

One wants to go on stoically believing—
As suits the long tradition of my people—
That all accept the Circle, and are brothers,
And through recital, all fulfill the cycle.
But no more are churches built with steeples pointing
Towards a cross within the clouds of Heaven.
Perhaps within this town, too many Christians
Exist, so that no room for yet another
Seems reasonable; better studied, better
Examined the indigenous persuasions
Of live humanity, than breathless letters.
For me, at least—and in this present darkness
In which I close my eyes, to find my vision
Has only clarified these abject senses,
To see ancestral memory's retrieval.
Perhaps this is my Patmos, and my exile.

Raised on Rogers

Gazing through this vintage house, I see
Hazy figures of the Cherokee,
Will Rogers, ceaselessly instructing me,

Through the seasons of my childhood,
Sending me out bravely to the wood,
Always with a wry word, on the good.

Those with bundled wood approve him, while
Ned Christie charms me with a semi-smile,
Near some territory's mercantile.

Once again, from sources I feared dead—
Oklahoma-born, but city-bred—
Uncle's repetitions fill my head

Like his filling, long ago, these halls
Sparingly with hide-clad, feathered dolls.
Hush contracts these rooms, when silence falls.

Though abandoned, with their pine studs bare,
Uncle's singing echoes everywhere:
"I dream of Jenny with the light brown hair . . ."

Tribal wisdom comes to me from sparrows
Flown above, like heads of living arrows,
Distant—though the gap between us narrows.

Ancient things return to me, by herds—
Bygone elk and buffalo. The birds
Bring again the elders' gentle words.

Now I have inherited this land,
Finally, I hear and understand
What they meant, by that reserved command

Graven on my anima from birth:
Hold to good, with all that you are worth;
Hold—though it be nothing but dry earth.

Cherokee Love Charm

<blockquote>An ancient Cherokee shaman's formula[1], translated</blockquote>

White Woman of the South, you drew close by,
And heard—astonishing to me below.
No one is ever lonely, when with you.
Along the path of purity you go,
A beauty slowly come to terrify.
You render me a white man instantly.
No one is ever lonely when with me.

You make the pathway white for me, and new,
Where dreariness will always fail to grow.
You place me there. It never will be blue.
The white road from above me, you bestow.
You've brought me from the high, white road, down low.
You place me in mid-earth, upright and free.
No one is ever lonely, when with me.

Attractively and handsome to the view,
You set me in the white house, place it so
It moves with me, where none is ever blue.
I'm in the house, wherever it may go.
With me, no one will ever suffer woe.
I never shall be blue, truthfully.
You bring it into being, instantly.

---

[1] On the color symbolism, "The spirit invoked is the White Woman, white being the color denoting the south. . . . [W]hite signifies peace and happiness, while blue is the emblem of sorrow and disappointment."—James Mooney, *Sacred Formulas of the Cherokees.*

Now, in the South, you've made the woman blue.
Along the path of blue, you've made her go.
Let her be veiled and lonely through and through.
Position her upon blue paths of snow,
Then bring her down to earth, from where her toe
Next touches, to wherever she may be,
Mark her with solitude, from Elahiyi.

Ha! I am very handsome, and I grew
Out of the Wolf Clan, which was long ago
Allotted to be intertwined with you,
Alone of all the clans allotted to
Make your oneness double into two,
Since the seven clans have come to be.
No one is ever lonely, when with me.

Allow our spirits to be intertwined,
So no one else is present in her mind.
Where every other man exists, there too
Is loneliness. The polecat and the crow
Alone will be their friends, so loathsome, so
Revolting are they, fitting company
For cuckoos' and opossums' misery.

Each of the seven clans is now a crew
To fill the soul with loneliness and woe,
And not at all good-looking, but a stew
Of refuse, clothed with dung, a sewage flow.
But I—I am ordained a white man, oh—
So-very-handsome, not, like them, debris.
Your soul has in the center entered me.

For I—I was ordained to be with you.
I stand, my face turned toward the Sun Land's glow,
A white man who will never turn to blue.
A shrouding house surrounds me, white as snow.
The white house comes wherever I may go
And covers me with light, eternally.
No one is ever lonely, when with me.

Not Quite Gods

I set a fire and sounded the alarm
As you arrived with gluttons, drunks, a whore
With poetry tattooed along her arm—
Like Big Guns riding in the days of yore;
Who forced your ways upon my simple kind,
Your popular perversions, lily-pale
And polled; your sicknesses of flesh and mind,
Promoted by the *Times*, through pony mail;
Rejecting us who scorn polluted arts
With shoulders cold—so privileged and so *bright*.

My brothers shot their shafts through your hard hearts
Inscrutably emerging from dark fir.
You lay, un-doctored dead men, then—not quite
The private, distant gods you thought you were.

Spearfinger

> ... too clumsy, too monstrous, too unnatural to be touched by the Poet ... the monstrous traditions of an uninteresting and, one may almost say, a justly exterminated race ... Indian legends, like Indian arrowheads, are well enough to hang up in cabinets for the delectation of the curious ...
> —Anonymous, "A Review of Longfellow's *The Song of Hiawatha*," *New York Times*, December 28, 1855

Grandmother oftentimes, dressed in her floral gown
And downy slippers, talked about that nearby town,

Chilhowie ("valley filled with deer" in Cherokee),
Which shares its name with a mountain found in Tennessee.

The Cherokee, before the tragic Trail of Tears,
Inhabited that country for eight hundred years.

They held a legend in that valley full of deer,
About a freak whose right forefinger was a spear.

How many centuries? One wonders. Who is counting?
This monster, for its refuge, chose Chilhowie Mountain.

Its body, with the density of ancient stone,
Adored to sit atop the barren crest alone—

Except one friend, the raven, whom it kept along,
To whom it sang—through fog and clouds—an eerie song.

It echoed from the peak, to reach the peaceful river:
"Uwe la na tsiku. Su sa sai: The liver,

I eat," It sang and danced atop Chilhowie's crest—
Its heart well-hidden in its wrist, not in its breast;

Protected by its hand, and undetected under
Its finger's spear, it beat to laughter loud as thunder.

The hunters of the Cherokee would lift their sight,
The boulders shifting wickedly, while birds took flight.

They warned the children not to trust an aging stranger—
"Utlunta prowls around the trails, a skilled shape-changer

Who knows your aunt's familiar form, and may appear,
To lure you near, and stab you with her right-hand spear.

Because she has a villager-grandmother's gait—
Stunted and shuffling, slow and limping—she will wait

Until she sees our forest fires, whose masking smoke
Allows her to slip past the gentle fairy folk,

Nunnehi, in her terrifying silver veil
Which curves around that blade she uses to impale.

Sharp as an onyx knife, and lengthy as a dagger,
And slender, as she slashes at the air, to stagger

And stare at its fair glint, and with a tired tread
Which tries for lightness, down the mountain she will thread,

Where fallen, roasted autumn chestnuts may be found
When Cherokees have burned the fall leaves on the ground.

Her blade beneath a blanket, to remain un-shown,
She waddles through their circle like some harmless crone,

Observing adolescent and ambitious tot,
As—gathering the ripened chestnuts, charred and hot—

The children pity her: "Here, have a chestnut, Granny.
Feeble elder, cross your ankles, rest your fanny . . ."

They settle on her lap, and quickly, she will kill
With one swift, expert puncture, in the harvest chill,

Extracting its gourmet reward—a liver young,
Refreshing, warm and tasteful to the morbid tongue.

She sings, "Uwe la na tsiku. Su sa sai,"
Which means, "The liver, I devour," in Cherokee.

To Lonely Lots

A rondeau entirely in Cherokee sounds

To lonely lots, you see a doe
Go slowly on a sunny quad,
To halt, to question you, to know—
You, next to equaling a god.
Among new leeks, on numbing snow,
To lonely lots.

"Ah, ha—you seek a soul. Hello,
Come, walk along. We glean," you nod,
"What's too hot-stalked. Talk—do you sow?
Doe, do you go to holy sod?"
Colloquially hum, "Yes? No?"
To lonely lots.

No geese sing to a yellow glow,
Yet sun must hunt some hollow clod.
Qualm to scuttle, wheat to stow,
To cue, to knot, to yoke, to wad . . .
Yet, see—she went a moon ago,
To lonely lots.

Made in America

Twelve bands of beads around each wrist,
Strange sun signs on my thighs,
I park the car and cross the lot,
No makeup to disguise.

A bag of oversized, faux-suede,
Deep taupe in color, dangles
From one square shoulder, fringed with strips
Which soften my hard angles.

Like Jo Jo in her blanket dress,
The Scottish miner's wife
Who calls to mind Chief Doublehead,
Who gave Grandfather life.

Below his throat a crucifix,
And seeming free from guile,
A man distracts me at the door,
To say he likes my style.

I start to say, "It's Indian."
Instead, I bite my lip,
And pull my turquoise chieftain tablet
Closer to my hip.

He sees it in the slanted glance
Above my high, sharp cheek—
Which flushes, it's so obvious,
I have no need to speak.

III. Blazing the Trail

Sapphics for Sequoyah

You, alone in history's fading ages
Ever known to code an uncharted language—
Bring me understanding, and bless my pages.
Hear me, Sequoyah!

Fashion red, square handkerchiefs, Crimson Hawk,
High above, and instantly come with red beads.
Round my throat—through which I attempt this small talk—
Drape them with brilliance.

Furnish me invention and novel wonder.
Lift my childish, Cherokee chin and answer.
Listen—though my grammar be garbled thunder,
After the lightning.

Ha! You see, a tree has been struck, is burning.
Shaman of my alphabet, dig a deep hole
At its base, filled with totemic learning,
yellow as stone slab.

Though I am impurity—low and little,
Pale as pennies laundered in bleach and sunshine—
Share with me possession of your thick spittle.
Let the relief come.

I Have No Drum

For Teddy—my Lonesome Bear

Return with snares of gut. I have no drum,
But you recall, each season of the crow,
I was the captain of the corps, and so—
A stick between four fingers and a thumb—
I cued commencement of the music show.
The cymbals trembled, while the Navajo
Would strike her bells. The rowdy would become
Respectful, introspective, moved and dumb.
Illini, Seminoles, and Chiefs would hum.
Inherited, within my blood, this rush
And rhythm, through its rude, inherent give
And take, seduces diehards to a hush,
And orients the lost, who once more live:
Led shrewdly, like a fox from foreign brush—
Primal and graceful, fine, yet primitive.

The Griffin

No immigration papers, ship, nor plane
To prove some place of Anglo origin,
They took a fine, Welsh surname, to explain
Away the tawny, thickened, native skin.

They left their birthplace, Carolina's north-
Most state, to emigrate, at twenty, west
Into southwest Virginia, then went forth
Into the Appalachian mountains, dressed

And civilized—fedoras pulled to brows
Revealing aboriginal descent,
To blend, then disappear, and never rouse
Suspicion as to where the Indians went.

My brilliant Griffin kin. What better word?
The sleek head of an eagle, with its span
Of wings—mythology's most sacred bird—
To indicate the subject of a clan.

I marvel at their savvy. "We're from Wales..."—
Unvoiced or voiced, with dignity and class,
To claim some foreign frigate raised its sails
And ferried us, allowing them to *pass*.

"The Welsh are dusky," I hear Samuel say,
Mahala in the cabin, pounding corn,
Heeding her husband's warning, "Keep away,
My dear, for you are clearly native-born."

He takes the ammunition and supplies
Beneath his muscular, bow-practiced arms,
Then smiles, a tortured twinkle in his eyes—
And who could overcome those tribal charms?

His first son coming in that very year
The Cherokee would be removed by force,
How prescient to remove himself, and here
Invent false fathers raised on hills of gorse.

No background, motion sickness, and no mast
Unnerving them across a hostile sea.
No scurvy, only character recast
That these mad interlopers leave them be.

Thus, bravely drinking trespass to its dregs,
They have bequeathed to me—their Griffin scion—
An eagle grafted on a wildcat's legs,
The body, brace and rudder of a lion.

I Have No Bow

For Teddy

Return with wood and string. I have no bow.
This, Uncle, only you could understand:
At fifteen, how they trusted to my hand
He-Who-Preserved-Our-People-Long-Ago;
And how I stood beside the Navajo
Upon a sweltering field of clay and sand,
Surrounded by a bare-armed, bare-legged band,
And drew my arrow straight, and let it go.
Return, and I will give you back the knife
Inlaid with carvings of wild river game
Arising from the waters, full of life.
Return, and call my daughter by the name
You gave her: *Katydid*. You have no wife
Nor child to keep you, as I raise and aim.

No Beatrice Am I

No Beatrice am I, a bride as bright
As Roman sun, to keep you always gold.
My words may not begin with "Lo! Behold..."
But follow me, and I will give you flight.
In me, the Red Man mingles with the White.
My trail is mine—inherited, twofold
In nature, and my *license* not controlled
By laws of men, but by another might.
I am a European thunderbird.
America was mine, from ancient ages.
I sing a harmony not ever heard.
Transcribe it, on your puritan white pages.
Like lush, twin, rushing rivers, I can hear it:
The red and blue blood, of the Great White Spirit.

Redfoot on the Trail of Tears

Many miles, flushed and shameful, did she walk,
Knowing neither where she was, nor where she went.
Dignified by want, she wandered, dry as chalk.

Song, her elder, like a shriveled cotton stalk,
Shrugged beside her, shuffling slowly, shoulders bent.
Many miles, flushed and shameful, did she walk.

Hearing white men whistle, watching black men gawk,
Fox, her father, forced to swallow his dissent,
Dignified by want, she wandered, dry as chalk.

Stiff as stone—a rolling stone through Little Rock—
Raven Mocker circling with depraved intent,
Many miles, flushed and shameful, did she walk.

Taunted by the memory of tomahawk,
Croatoan moan and Chickasaw lament,
Dignified by want, she wandered, dry as chalk.

So I see her go—with small but valiant talk—
West, while I lie low within the ones unsent,
Many miles, flushed and shameful, did she walk,
Dignified by want. She wandered, dry as chalk.

How Many Perished?

How many Griffins perished on that Trail
We call in Cherokee, "Road where they cried,"
Our braves turned burning red, the elders pale?

No count remains, of female or of male.
They fell, and they were buried where they died.
How many Griffins perished on that Trail?

How many troops forbade my kin to wail,
Commanding, like the corn, their tears be dried?
Our braves turned burning red, the elders, pale.

Few names survive. How many others fail?
Charles, Daniel, Jane, and John each walked beside
Our braves, turned burning red, the elders, pale.

For all their substance, who would not prevail?
The losses do not speak—but are implied.
How many Griffins perished on that Trail?

Like hay straws, bound and dumped, bale after bale,
Their last rites from a shaman's lips denied,
How many Griffins perished on that Trail—
Our braves turned burning red, our elders, pale?

Five Fly Skyward

Five fly skyward, ruffled, puffing,
Like the flight of friend on friend;
Puffy bodies roughly buffing
Heaven, when ten more descend.

What a service, what requital!
These are those I once considered
Less ephemeral than vital,
And for whom my time was frittered?

Greener than the green of Greenwich
Village silk which willow dart
Moths consume—the tint of spinach—
Grows my sight as each departs.

Though, as I observe the sequel
Blown in flocks out of the blue,
Each seems greater than its equal—
Swifter, fairer, and more true.

Tired Blood to Colonel Hawthorne

My blanket, Colonel Hawthorne—where shall I
Unroll its "forbidden" fibers, smooth, and spread
These corners formed of diamond-patterned thread,
To make my bed, for good or ill, and lie?
Piece after piece, my every dwelling, my
Every stretch for resting, you possess and tread,
And take the fields, to hunt until they're dead
My bulls, believing they are yours to buy.
Where would you see me banished, having taken
This country which is mine, to give me naught?
Where shall I go? Where would you have me waken?
All of my rightful regions, you have bought—
You and your sort, who own the bile to ravage
The ever-generous and trusting savage.

This Primitive Rain Dance

No, darling, no—I can't pick up the phone
Just yet, for neither business nor romance.
I cannot run the ever-present chance
Your tone might prove a sling, your heart, unknown,
Knifed at me through the wires. If, left alone,
I thrive, recalling how—at your first glance—
You fell, realize the primitive rain dance
Is done to douse the potent firestone.

I need you as the maple needs the sun.
I love you as the grizzly loves her young.
I want you as free spirits want a choice;
Pursued by past transgressions, though, I run,
Terrified tenderness has left your tongue,
Afraid again of damage from that voice.

Angry Indian Lover

My angry Indian lover—peace, be calm.
Come, loose the leather round your narrow hips.
Relinquish what sits hidden in your palm,
And let me press against your bowstring lips
My own.
        Come—lay aside your evil scheme,
And open on my own your brutal mouth.
You are my dream arising from a dream,
My answer from the Woman of the South.

Allow me to retrace the diverse shades
Of red and yellow running through each calf.

Unwind and spread across my chest your braids.

My angry Indian lover, come and laugh.

White Pocahontas

Their jaws will drop, I know, as in we walk
And there will be no peace until we leave—
But life lasts merely moments. Let them talk,
For later on will come my calm reprieve.
Their heads will turn, I know, as we walk in.
The maître d' will seat us, while they mumble.
But beauty will not stay, so let them spin.
I'll bow my head, as penitent and humble
As I know how to be. What they don't know;
What, darling, they don't understand, I do.
They see me as the redskin, mixed-breed doe,
Though what these wealthy patrons want is you.
My native name—bizarre to them as Greek—
These cowboys covet, but they never speak.

The Water Cannibals

A Cherokee legend

Before the dawn arrives, arise,
Your weariness—however deep—
Swabbed absolutely from your eyes,
With all the vestiges of sleep.

The demons search for sluggish flesh
By daylight—whether sweet or sour,
Uncaring whether old or fresh—
And, like the woodland wolves, devour.

Destroying children, maids, and men
Alike, with ghostly arrows they
Transport to death the laggard, then
To beds of river, stream, or bay;

To leave a dummy in their place
Which knows the way to act and speak
And fool the tribe, who find the face
Convincing, for another week.

Arise and string your bow, get dressed.
You saw them coming, all along.
Though black clouds blow out of the west,
These devils must be proven wrong.

Arise, get dressed, and string your bow
Before Sun rises in the east—
Unlike the dreamer dragged below,
Who shall, in liquid, be their feast.

Wounded Knee

Bury my heart, which still must beat,
With acid soil, and white deceit,
And let it feed a foot of wheat,

Before I buckle—red and tender—
Discrediting my race and gender
By unconditional surrender.

Were I to make the treaty good,
What wilderness, in totem, should
Be given me, of western wood?

That savage attribute, Surprise,
Appraises Little Big Horn lies
From hidden heights beneath the skies.

Once while I stood in stormy weather,
Drawing my spade and hands together
Firmly in gloves of doe-skin leather,

Between slim rows of squash and corn,
Planting long lines of fire thorn,
Something sublime in me was born.

All I possess, all that remains,
Is but to scoop the bandits' brains,
Like brute Comanches on the plains,

Returning to the sacred dust,
And the Great Spirit as I must.
When none submit, who dares to trust?

Ka No Gi S Di Asks the Amorous Commander

Divested of the leathers of first daughter
For recompense, what gift should I require
Once you have doused with scorn and firewater
My fathers, clad in gentlemen's attire?
Two feathers and a squirrel's tail, says the Jackson
Distinguishing the Red Sticks from my kind.
In autumn fields of Creeks flayed by the flaxen,
What brotherhood should I expect to find?
Beneath me on these leaves of brown and rust,
I know it is impossible to speak.
You see, I am an enemy to trust
Despite the love and hate which make you weak.
In drops and lines of visionary red,
Tecumseh's hand draws blood around my bed.

To Melissa Honey Bee, Who Has Hidden My Feathers in a Dream

No sorrow would I feel, had they been arrows.
Such weapons would be easily replaced
By virtue of their fletcher's measures, traced
With ease, and found in native caves or barrows.
But the Great Spirit's eye is on the sparrows
And the Good Fletcher's hand itself has graced
Those hollow quills which fly more true, and placed
Escape from human sin within their marrows.
Without it—hear me, Sister—I will perish;
So while this prank may be an awful dream
Made by some midnight devil to torment me,
And while you share no love for what I cherish
(Your character not cruel as it might seem),
You take what He—to save my life—has sent me.

I Have No Horse

For Teddy

Return with racing hooves. I have no horse,
For long ago, I gave away the stable
You bought for me. I had become unable
To work them to a lather on the course.

Recall with fond approval, how each fall
And winter, through till spring, the Navajo
And I were so responsible, to go
And empty every steed and pony's stall,

To ride and ride, around those steep and slick
Layers in the land, where Man had dug
To strip it of its riches, with a shrug—
In order that his sons had salt to lick.

Come back with two strong stallions we can ride—
O brother of my mother, Lonesome Bear—
Or I would be as happy with a mare,
As long as she keeps steady, and in stride.

On a Plane Going East

For Papaw

How proud you'd be to witness this, how proud,
My walker of the wind, you who would build
The scrapers for New York, completely thrilled
With pride, to watch me walk above a cloud.
I fly towards the rising rays which gild
My bird's white wings, its underbelly filled
With shadow, like an eagle's dragging shroud
Around its talons, down, no fear allowed.
I fly no longer on the mourning dove,
But on descent, at whose first tremors, I,
Losing altitude, gain balance by your love.
Upon steel beams you wait to catch me, high
Above your scrutinizing eyes, above
The opening you scraped within the sky.

Half-breed

Both sides accepted me, both sides denied.
Each side has told me truth, while each has lied.

Unite two liquids in a cup of clay,
Their properties do not congeal and stay.

No more is it half-water and half-wine,
But each absorbs the other, to combine.

Its drops are wine and water, through and through,
But yet dissimilar, completely new.

My blood—all Indian while still all white—
Mixes and balances, a dual birthright.

I am your bridge. I am, as well, your breach.
Hear me, and heal—I'm none of you, and each.

The Jealous She-Raccoon among Garbage Cans

Sphinx moths amass, the bandit night is young,
But no one has invited me inside.
The taste of bobcat lingers on my tongue,
A predator. The things I have to hide!
Observing cold, contrary crossing stars,
Behold the brilliant scavenger—my rotten
Eggs consumed with truffles, caviars.
How I would thrill to fill her mouth with cotton
Candy, make her ride the clever cat
If only one long, vulgar time, to kill
This persevering cord. That would be that—
Feel nothing, neither good will nor ill will.
The wild is no suggested place to care.
If fright may threaten love . . . *not there, not there.* . . .

On an Antique Photograph of My Martin Aunts

Eleven vintage ladies faintly smile,
So aboriginal in shade and face,
Their bobbed hair and their European style
Of dress look either forced or out of place.

The central figure strikes an easy pose,
Rail-thin and angular and flat of chest.
I see my bushy brows, triangular nose,
the attitude in which I, too, am dressed.

Front row, one rounds her back and leans—a charmer
With ducked chin, depth so strong, she might be black
Instead of Siouan; clothed for staying warmer
In long, dark sleeves the light-garbed others lack.

Attentive and—though pleasant—each intense
As lasers in the bright, Missouri glare,
They show my soul to me, with that stark sense
Which fills the Indian's hundred-yard-long stare.

Navajo and Cherokee

Bemused, removed, and cool, they watched us go—
Two little Indians of copper, we—
Forbidden from their white society:
You, the purebred "Latin" Navajo,
I, the paler, cross-breed Cherokee,
A pinto* with my roots round Tennessee,
From origins I couldn't let you see,
Who spoke with spirits which refused to show.
My closest friend, you never knew! You never
Imagined, as they killed you by degrees,
With each repellent rumor, every jibe,
Envying you, so nimble and so clever,
So beautiful and so inclined to please—
The tallest and most noble of our tribe.

*pinto: pejorative term for a mixed blood Caucasian/Native American

IV. Homeland

At Cahokia Indian Mounds

At fourteen years of age, past rain-filled ruts
One hundred feet in height, my father climbed
This mound—an eager scout with Osage blood.
Around him spread wild brush, chill Illinois
Unknown and still, in silence spilling blooms
Of yellow dandelion, where he slept.
Then all the questions—spoken yet unanswered
Remained: how had this mountain come to be?
The mysteries, like rabbits, multiplied—
A metaphor of his identity.
These Borrow Pits were yet to be discovered,
The reservoirs of earth to be transported
By baskets woven well, no beast of burden
Nor wheeled machine to ease the carrier.
And here I stand—my leatherhide, fringed bag
So heavy hanging from my sharp, square shoulder—
A wooden flute in hand, got from my father.
In merely twenty years, they built this mound!
And here I stand, atop the flat fourth terrace,
Upon the grassy plain the ancient temple
Once occupied. I climbed the steps to Heaven,
Two steep-cut flights, where Father had to clamber,
And wonder without answers. Stoic, blue
And wind-blown, I—with Siouan attitude—
Absorb the energy from what lies buried
Below, but at my native being, stirs.

No vivid diorama then existed
Through which my father might have closed the circle,
His ancient people in that habitat
Where biting flies draw blood. O mothers! Fathers!
See, I have come! Reward me with some vision.
If not this, then the words, to bring it forth.

For when I have returned to sow with pumpkin
My low, subtropic field, to fertilize
The corn, and stake the Cherokee tomatoes,
These acres will be new again with children
Who chatter in attentively, who wander
Across these sacred spaces, unattended—
Accompanied by no one but each other—
While I revisit you, alone and grown.

Profaning with an artificial swish
From pant and yellow jacket, like a hornet,
Some adolescent will obstruct that passage
Into the Osage sky, from one like me.
Some jogger wearing glasses and a ball cap
Again will use these white memorial markers
For push-ups! Breathe in slowly, soul, breathe out,
And pace yourself, my heart—for in the long run,
This shirt of olive green and flute of wood
Make good the least authentic memory.

Aqua, Turquoise, and Teal

Aqua, turquoise, and teal
Always were present within—
Colors to calm and to heal,
Flattering yellow-red skin;

Hues to dissolve and unharden,
Hidden or brought to the fore—
Under the Lord in the garden,
Next to the cherry front door;

Over the chair of tan buck,
Framing some Great Smoky lake—
Teal like the rings of a duck,
Teal like the down of a drake.

Aqua in undisturbed water,
Next to wreathed platters of thatch;
Sewn on the dress of a daughter,
Threaded through pocket and patch.

Clothing a spoon or a lighter,
Turquoise was spread on the table—
Proven to focus the writer,
Making one mentally stable.

Aqua, turquoise, and teal:
Stone, and the sky, and the sea.
Opposite, on the wise wheel,
Color as copper as we.

The Rivers of the Navajo

> The toxic mine waste of heavy metals in the San Juan River, from an accident caused by the US Environmental Protection Agency at the Gold King Mine in Colorado, is an assault on Navajo culture and life.
> — Alastair Lee Bitsoi, "Council reacts to report on Gold King spill," *Navajo Times*, August 10, 2015

Despite the glowing glory of its course—
The falcon challenged, and the raven raced—
It threatens eighty miles, from its source
At King's Mine, with three hundred tons of waste.

Seen from that falcon's flight, the filth portends
A foe, from which these reapers gather doom—
These farmers of the feather—at both ends
To which the river drags its yellow plume.

From Shiprock, giving early Morning Prayer
For corn, and squash, and melons to deliver,
To Cement Creek, that tributary where
El Río de las Ánimas—the River

Of Souls—has been made poison, which will last
For decades still to be. Perhaps, indeed,
Those streams will not be clean, till I have passed
To Heaven's happy buffalo stampede.

How much of Earth, within one day, may die,
And never be recovered—but behold!
While governments avoid, delay, and lie,
The rivers of the Navajo run gold!

And none may handle them, till heavy metal
Of arsenic, cadmium, copper, tin, and lead
Commingle in a weight of care which settles
Cemented to its sacred, naked bed.

Beyond my seat and site, beyond my scope
Of reasoning, beyond my reach, beyond
My problem—yet it is within my hope
To offer hope, beside my thriving pond.

Who am I, but a comrade to the daughter
Of Baca, loaning her my bow and arrow?—
Affected deeply by the rape of water,
Corpuscles white, with crimson red bone marrow.

Weep with the Waters

> The US Environmental Protection Agency, which had inadvertently caused the spill of three million gallons of mineral-rich water into the Animas River last Wednesday while remediating an abandoned mine near Silverton, Colorado, was working with the Navajo Nation to bring clean water to farmers along the San Juan so they could irrigate their crops and water their animals.
> —*Navajo Times*, August 2015

Weep with the San Juan waters, sisters,
    Far from their flowing, row,
Passing the cactus, as August blisters
    Native and Navajo;

Carrying with you, fleet and flustered,
    Children to see these scenes—
Poisonous currents like yellow mustard—
    Children who carry genes

Hundreds of years in maternal making.
    Show them—but do not drink.
Smile, while your parted heart is breaking,
    Watching your fortunes shrink:

Lest you contract a pale-faced sickness,
    Catching some dull disease.
Cover your skin, and thank its thickness.
    Shelter its agencies.

Weep for the offices and hands
    Of presidents priced to sell;
Not for the sacred, stolen lands,
    Nor for the toxic well.

Weep for the white man's lust for gold,
    Not for the withered clover.
Think of the lessons to be told,
    Once their affair is over.

Song of the Long-Hair Clan

Excluded as the snowflake is from spring,
And fading from the fields and plains like flowers,
We bring to you, False Friends, a fresher thing.

We read your talking leaves. Their edicts sting
Our ears, our dignity, which bolts and sours,
Excluded as the snowflake is from spring.

But see—for you, we do not cease to sing,
Prevented from that status rightly ours.
We bring to you, False Friends, a fresher thing.

Like you, as worshipful and worshipping,
But unlike you—who revel in your powers—
Excluded as the snowflake is from spring,

We keep tradition, peace. The pipe will ring
With music, though we drown in March's showers.
We bring to you, False Friends, a fresher thing.

We call it "what is real." Its coloring
Perplexes, as attested by your glowers—
Excluded as the snowflake is from spring.
We bring to you, False Friends, a fresher thing.

In Tulsa

In Tulsa, every setting sun—
    A stranger from the last—
Surprises and unsettles one
    With vivid ribbons cast.

Horizons lathed and volatile
    Invite the whirlwinds down
To meet the new Chief Principal,
    With funnels throughout town

That leave Apache-brown the narrow
    Paths they have unearthed
In Tahlequah and Broken Arrow,
    Like twin babies birthed.

And the Great Spirit winds and speaks
    In ways one never hears
On the Great Smoky Mountain peaks
    To the same native ears.

The Man of Mystery from the West,
    In feathers of crow black,
May not approve you as his guest,
    And greet you with attack.

To cleanse the soil, he may chase
    And turn an ashen shade
A politician's pallid face
    Who crosses it, in trade,

Returning to the Seventh Height
    To let the funnels rage,
Which—ever in a different light—
    Preserve there a New Age.

Supply Package for Sacred Stone Camp

To the Standing Rock Sioux in protest

Nine hairnets, and a scarlet sleeping bag;
Two tribal tie-downs, fastened round a tarp
I send you, with a North Dakota tag—
Nothing toxic, flammable, or sharp.

Two tribal tie-downs, fastened round a tarp
To waterproof your teepee from the rain.
Nothing toxic, flammable, or sharp
To poison, nor addict you, nor cause pain.

To waterproof your teepee from the rain,
Accept my silver "quilt." I have not come
To poison, nor addict you, nor cause pain.
These nets will only hold the hair of some.

Accept my silver "quilt." I have not come
With nets enough for all of you, of course.
These nets will only hold the hair of some,
In case you fall in protest from your horse.

With nets enough for all of you, of course,
I might protect your precious scalps from harm
In case you fall in protest from your horse.
I send this scarlet bag, to keep you warm.

I might protect your precious scalps from harm,
From rocks and bugs upon that sacred ground.
I send this scarlet bag, to keep you warm
While you defend the water which is wound

Throughout us and around us, and is life.
Nine hairnets and a scarlet sleeping bag—
No bow, gun, mace, fierce animal, or knife—
I send you, with a North Dakota tag.

A Sioux Protest

Not since the Little Big Horn have the seven
Dispersed, outnumbered, bittersweet Sioux bands
Been wholly reunited under Heaven
To guard the dignity of sacred lands.

Machines, black lettered yellow, doze their plains
Outside the reservation's grassy border—
But none apologizes or explains
For these disturbances of Nature's order.

A serpent underground, transporting oil
From east to west, is what they want to lay.
The natives' sediment is merely soil,
Their holy bones, mere fossils in the way.

As engines grind and gears engage, a crowd
Assembles. Skyward winds a woman's wail.
But here, no peaceful protest is allowed.
The pauper's place for questioning is jail.

Before emotion may be disengaged,
It first must be acknowledged. As it clogs
The nearby campground, one sees young and aged.
The Company lets loose aggressive dogs—

Their savage handlers cold and all—all—white.
As blood drips from a panting shepherd's tongue,
A child and pregnant woman feel the bite.
Another, sprayed with stinging mace, is flung

With roughness to the ground, her arms jerked back
Behind her. There appears a painted horse.
At no time do the Indians attack.
No need exists for this excessive force,

Except that of weak souls, which seek excuse
For "Progress"—the first name of Exploitation.
Who furthers "evolution" through abuse
Deserves the scorn of native, tribe, and nation.

V. Prophesies

The Chosen One

Someone somewhere said, "Someday, a son
Or daughter will be free enough and brave
Enough to sing our music, and to save
Our themes—when our Great Spirit, too, will stun
Those ears that hear, and when their eyes will run
With tears, at this sure harmony we gave,
To sorrow, that they chased us to the grave."

Then I said: "Let me be that Chosen One."
My elders were unanimously sober,
As though they had provoked me, I remember.
Black Davis nodded. Great Grandmother Song
Suggested I arrive in late October,
One sun before the first moon of November—
For in the Fall, the Fallen Ones belong.

The Arrowhead

She speaks to me. Once more, I come apart.
He cautions, "She will never be your friend.
This is her standard pretense and pretend,
The arrowhead which precedes the poison dart.
She is a wet, world-famous work of art—
But beauty will not save you in the end.
Hers is no word on which you can depend,
But was your adversary, from the start."
He says, "Remain my Shenandoah spy,
Indigenous and real—my running brave,
Outfitted in the skins of buck and doe—
My mockingbird, born with a falcon's eye.
Refuse the English queen who would enslave,
And flee the 'friend' who is a native foe."

They Won't Remove Me

They won't remove me. I will still be left
Below these hills, to breathe this chilly air,
Instilled with wonder—wary and aware,
Feather-weighted, leather-dressed and deft;

And further—I will be her stare, her heft,
The color and the cowlick in her hair,
And when she sees herself, I shall be there
Within her trembling chin, fixed in its cleft.

They won't remove me—never will they take
Me, live nor dead. I sleep, when she will wake.
I am the man behind her female mask,
A fourth of firewater in her flask.

We call ourselves, "The-People-Who-Are-Real"
On grounds these thieves are powerless to steal.

We Told You So

They come. They say, "We told you so.
Tired Blood—hear our counsel now.
Relinquish nothing of yourself.
Exchange no name, and make no vow.

The bare, gray bur oak you revere
along your lonely, daily trek
from which suspend those ticklish globes
against the sky, each one a speck,

will strengthen you, and, too, inspire,
will comfort you, as we will guide.
Precious one—we will not mislead.
We are your house. In us, abide."

Come to me, Song and Running Stream,
in Nature's clothing—neutral, mute.
My toe breaks through my moccasin.
My heel has crushed the bur oak's fruit.

And dusk has come, my confidant,
bringing the shade in which you're safe.
And here I watch and wait, your child,
your grandchild—wasting, long-haired waif.

Red Jacket to the Seneca, on Religion

Brothers!—Be formal, somber-jawed and stiff.
Dozens of Black Coats walk among our people,
Eager to whip you when they catch a whiff
Of weakness, drag you screaming to their steeple.

Brothers!—they will berate you with a Book,
Claiming its truth within, but can't agree,
All of them, how to walk it. They, who took
Mountain and meat and simple faith from ye!

Brothers!—we beg them: leave us out of trouble.
Make your minds easy, tend your duties first.
Otherwise, with too much, our heads may bubble,
By and by overloaded, till they burst!

Rinse My Sins

No longer can I stand these heavy rattles
Of turtle shell tied tightly to my shins.
Baptize me, in between your British battles,
And make the sacred liquid rinse my sins.
The bath will not eradicate this running
Of pigment in my skin, nor render clean
The red clay of my flesh, for all the cunning
Of Cleopatra—your exotic queen
From whom my mother takes her "Christian" name,
And thus, this stain, as though I roast in flame.
Remove these bracelets of beaded teal
Your fairer women beg, borrow, strip, or steal.
Pretend I am a blonde, full-blooded daughter.
Hey-yah, hey-yah, hey-yah. Prepare the water.

A Wail from the Wild Potato Clan Arbor

Which one will ever know of this and value you?
"No one, no one, not ever," vows the mockingbird.
"No one, no one, forever. Every pretty word
Will serve to praise another in your place," they coo.
"Unnoted till the end of time," intones the shrew.
The pewter wings of pigeons wave—"Unheard, unheard!"
A feather is dispersed each beat as air is stirred.
"Not only now but evermore. Adieu! Adieu!"
"Because you chose the rose-free, thorn-inviting road,"
The stones admonish me, "your role will be forgotten . . . "
"Forgotten, yes!" picks up and croaks the moldy toad.
The mushrooms of the forest, too—spore-marked and rotten—
Spit disapproval in my face, and then explode
Within my gathered skirt, to scorch its orchid cotton.

The Flute My Father Gave

Dew through the chamber, a route blue with sorrow,
Suing the air of the autumn with sounds,
Found at the ancient Cahokia mounds,
Rueful, the tune from my flute soaks tomorrow.

Doomed and acute as a fire pit fuming,
Cinders consuming wherever they fall,
Five fluid notes toll askew like a ball—
Fading, renewing, bemusing, resuming.

Who could refuse, of those few in the forest
Fated to me, while the friendly new moon
Fools the rude fox, falcon, squirrel and raccoon?
Who would choose muteness, from finest to poorest?

Chute like the lovesick Lakota's for wooing,
Floods the nude view with its flutters, to brood
Fiercely, with full but forlorn attitude—
Prudently, simple astuteness accruing.

They Won't Erase Me

They won't erase me, not the slightest part,
Nor bleach these features, nor withhold from me
The consciousness of this identity
Which quarters, by the quart, in my red heart.
And neither will its regulated art—
So like primeval drumming—be pried free
From that acknowledged Qualla Boundary
Within whose woods the fires of status start.
My eyes aslant, these vandals shall be faced,
All chambers of my heart, with culture, filled;
A profile reticent to be erased—
Willing to blur, before it would be killed,
Accepting of the truth, however slight,
White print is worthless, when the page is white.

How to Hide the Native

Purchase powder pale as milk,
With names like "Marble, Level One."
The copper common to your ilk
Is rarer than cosmetic sun.

Line kohl of coffee brown or ash
With wider thickness as it goes
Along the lower, outer lash,
To make your eyes round as the doe's;

In hopes perhaps no more will tease
The children—without pang or guilt—
Who chuckle, with, "Are you Chinese?
Do you have Down's? Your eyes—they tilt."

Sweep shadow in Apache Gold
Just over your near-lidless crease,
To cloak the epicanthic fold,
Pronounced as that of Chief Cochise.

One day, your shame shall turn to pride—
Or more like dignifying grace—
When alabaster Genocide
Wails, as you raise your reddened face.

Cherokee Childbirth Chant

> An ancient Cherokee shaman's formula, translated

Hey little boy, hey little boy,
Do not be slow, do not be slow,
Come out, come out, what can it be?
Hey little boy, do not be slow.
It is a bow, it is a bow.
Let's see who gets it, see who gets it,
See who gets it, come and see...

Hey little girl, hey little girl,
Do not be slow, do not be slow,
Come out, come out, what can it be?
Hey, little girl, do not be slow;
A colander, a colander.
Let's see who gets it, see who gets it,
See who gets it, come and see...

The Charts and Wheels

The charts and wheels with reason reassure
Me steadily that you and I are one,
By quark and quasar, symbol, sign, and sun,
Till—like the true believer—I endure
Their catechisms: no love is more pure
Than this, no fury more fantastic, none
More ruling, unrelenting and mature.
For you, I shift in shape, and drop my role,
Deciphering each synergistic dream.
Removed from proof, conceit and self-control
Lie practices I've pushed to an extreme,
Till I have let the double of my soul
Appear intangible as legends seem.

O Great Spirit

Great Spirit of the God who is alive,
Whose risen Son I seek before the dawn,
Who makes the black and gold sunflower thrive,
The earthworm loosen soil beneath the lawn;
Great Spirit, grant my late grandmothers' looks
Attend me while I rub her cherry hutch.
Great Spirit, grant my late grandfather's books
Preserve his signature I love to touch.
Surround and show to me that massive cloud
Of witnesses—undauntable or docile.
Allow their countenances to enshroud
My shoulders, spoken of by Your Apostle.
Send generous *Nunnehi* to my steeple,
Returning me, at last, to my dark people.

Benediction

May the warmth of Heaven
On your home bestow soft air,
Grant that the Great Spirit
Bless all who enter there.
May your moccasins
Make glad tracks in countless snows,
And always on your shoulder
May rain bestow its bows.

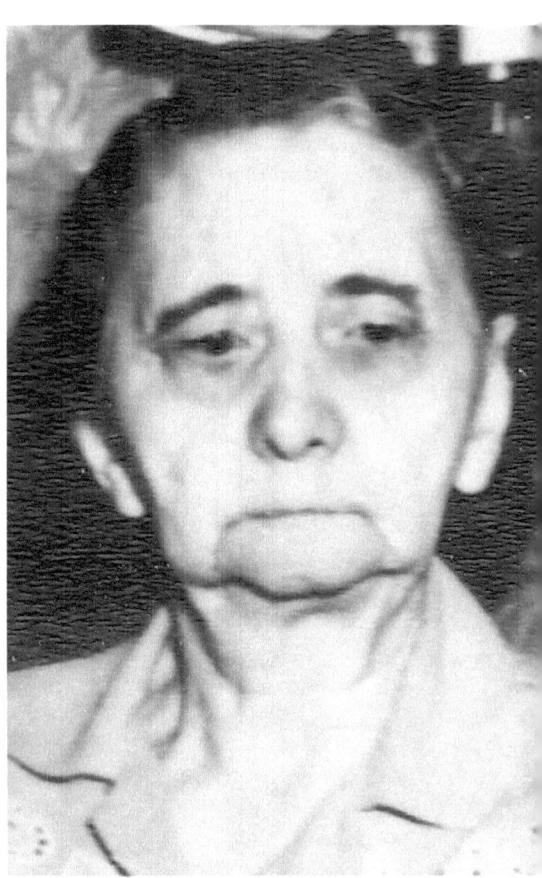

Notes

The sacred formulas here translated are representative of more than six hundred Cherokee prayers, formulas, and songs, which were collected on the Cherokee reservation in North Carolina in 1887 and 1888, recorded by anthropologist and ethnographer, James Mooney.

Notes on the Photographs:

page vi: The author's Amerindian maternal grandfather, to whom this collection is dedicated, and who appears in many poems.

page 122, left: The author's Amerindian maternal great-grandmother, Griffin, referenced in the poem, "Made in America."
right: The author's Amerindian maternal great-great-aunt, Minnie Griffin.

page 123: The author's Amerindian paternal great-great-aunts, Martin, from Joshua Martin, referenced in multiple poems.

page 124, left: The author's Amerindian maternal great-great-uncle, William Griffin, and wife.
right: The author's Amerindian maternal great-aunt, Novella Maiden.

page 125, left: The author's Amerindian maternal uncle, Ted (Teddy, "Lonesome Bear," referenced numerous times in this collection), with his horse.
right: The author's Amerindian paternal great-grandmother, Ora, referenced in several poems.

page 126, left: The author's Amerindian paternal grandfather, Stanley Potts, Sr., referenced in the poem, "Black Flies and Berries."
right: Amerindian grandmother of the author's paternal grandfather. Civil War era, original tintype. Early photographic portrait of a Native American Indian, Christian convert.

JENNIFER REESER is the author of five collections of poetry. Her first, *An Alabaster Flask*, was the winner of the Word Press First Book Prize. X. J. Kennedy wrote that her debut "ought to have been a candidate for a Pulitzer." Her third, *Sonnets from the Dark Lady and Other Poems*, was a finalist for the Donald Justice Prize. Her fourth, *The Lalaurie Horror*, debuted as an Amazon bestseller in the category of Epic Poetry.

Reeser's poems, reviews, and translations of Russian, French, along with the Cherokee and various Native American Indian languages, have appeared in *POETRY, Rattle*, the *Hudson Review, Recours au Poème, LIGHT Quarterly*, the *Formalist*, the *Dark Horse, SALT, Able Muse*, and elsewhere. Her poetry has been anthologized in Random House London's *Everyman's Library* Series, in Longman's *Introduction to Poetry*, in the *Hudson Review*'s historic *Poets Translate Poets*, and in others.

A biracial writer of Anglo-Celtic and Native American Indian ancestry, Reeser was born in Louisiana. She studied English at McNeese State University in Lake Charles, Louisiana, and also in Tulsa, Oklahoma, her former home.

Reeser is the former assistant editor of *Iambs & Trochees*, as well as a former moderator, manuscript consultant, and mentor with the West Chester Poetry Conference.

Reeser's translations of the Russian poet Anna Akhmatova are

approved by Akhmatova's living heir, and authorized by her agents in Moscow.

Reeser received her first writing award from the Pulitzer Prize winner, Robert Olen Butler, while in high school. She has received the Poets Respond Prize from *Rattle*, the Innovative Form Award from the World Order of Narrative and Formalist Poets, as well as the Lyric Memorial Prize and the New England Prize. Reeser's work has been nominated seven times for the Pushcart Prize, and numerous times for the *Best of the Net* anthology; and her work has been set to music by the classical/art song composer, Lori Laitman, for her tribute to writer Edna St. Vincent Millay. Reeser's poems have been translated into Urdu, Hindi, Persian, and Czech. Her website is www.jenniferreeser.com.

Also from Able Muse Press

Jacob M. Appel, *The Cynic in Extremis – Poems*

William Baer, *Times Square and Other Stories;*
New Jersey Noir – A Novel

Lee Harlin Bahan, *A Year of Mourning (Petrarch) – Translation*

Melissa Balmain, *Walking in on People (Able Muse Book Award for Poetry)*

Ben Berman, *Strange Borderlands – Poems;*
Figuring in the Figure – Poems

Lorna Knowles Blake, *Green Hill (Able Muse Book Award for Poetry)*

Michael Cantor, *Life in the Second Circle – Poems*

Catherine Chandler, *Lines of Flight – Poems*

William Conelly, *Uncontested Grounds – Poems*

Maryann Corbett, *Credo for the Checkout Line in Winter – Poems;*
Street View – Poems

John Philip Drury, *Sea Level Rising – Poems*

Rhina P. Espaillat, *And After All – Poems*

Anna M. Evans, *Under Dark Waters: Surviving the* Titanic *– Poems*

D. R. Goodman, *Greed: A Confession – Poems*

Margaret Ann Griffiths, *Grasshopper – The Poetry of M A Griffiths*

Katie Hartsock, *Bed of Impatiens – Poems*

Elise Hempel, *Second Rain – Poems*

Jan D. Hodge, *Taking Shape – carmina figurata;*
The Bard & Scheherazade Keep Company – Poems

Ellen Kaufman, *House Music – Poems*

Carol Light, *Heaven from Steam – Poems*

Kate Light, *Character Shoes – Poems*

April Lindner, *This Bed Our Bodies Shaped – Poems*

Martin McGovern, *Bad Fame – Poems*

Jeredith Merrin, *Cup – Poems*

Richard Moore, *Selected Poems;*
        Selected Essays

Richard Newman, *All the Wasted Beauty of the World – Poems*

Alfred Nicol, *Animal Psalms – Poems*

Frank Osen, *Virtue, Big as Sin (Able Muse Book Award for Poetry)*

Alexander Pepple (Editor), *Able Muse Anthology;*
        Able Muse – a review of poetry, prose & art (semiannual, winter 2010 on)

James Pollock, *Sailing to Babylon – Poems*

Aaron Poochigian, *The Cosmic Purr – Poems;*
        Manhattanite (Able Muse Book Award for Poetry)

John Ridland, *Sir Gawain and the Green Knight (Anonymous) – Translation*
        Pearl (Anonymous) – Translation

Stephen Scaer, *Pumpkin Chucking – Poems*

Hollis Seamon, *Corporeality – Stories*

Ed Shacklee, *The Blind Loon: A Bestiary*

Carrie Shipers, *Cause for Concern (Able Muse Book Award for Poetry)*

Matthew Buckley Smith, *Dirge for an Imaginary World (Able Muse Book Award for Poetry)*

Barbara Ellen Sorensen, *Compositions of the Dead Playing Flutes – Poems*

Rosemerry Wahtola Trommer, *Naked for Tea – Poems*

Wendy Videlock, *Slingshots and Love Plums – Poems;*
        The Dark Gnu and Other Poems;
        Nevertheless – Poems

Richard Wakefield, *A Vertical Mile – Poems*

Gail White, *Asperity Street – Poems*

Chelsea Woodard, *Vellum – Poems*

www.ablemusepress.com

www.ingramcontent.com/pod-product-compliance
Lightning Source LLC
Chambersburg PA
CBHW020333170426
43200CB00006B/373